Practise
Handwriting

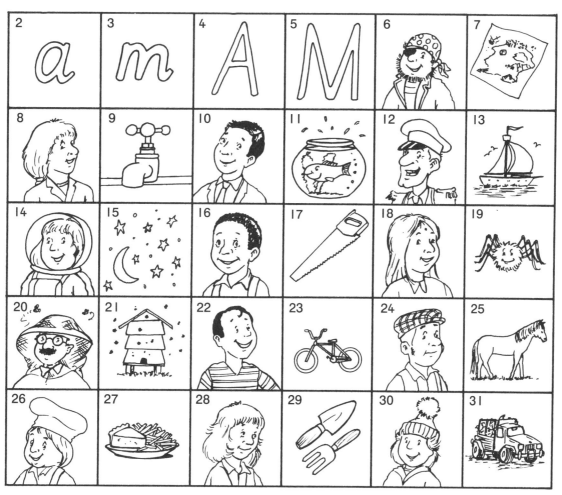

Colour each picture as you finish each page.

Written by Jillian Harker and Geraldine Taylor
Illustrated by Andrew Everitt-Stewart
Calligraphy by Maureen Hallahan

Letter formation

Copy these letters.

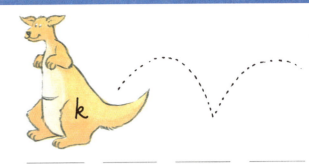

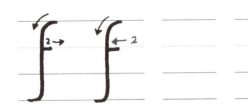 

↓m
↓n
↙o
↓p
↙q²
↓r
↙s

↓t²   ↓t←²
↓u²
↓v
↓w
✗²
↓y²↓
⇢z⇢

Parent point: By the time your child starts school, you will know if she* is right or left-handed. You will make it easier for a left-hander if you show how to form certain letters of the alphabet her special way. Left-handers should look for the grey arrows on these pages. Keep plenty of spare paper handy for extra practice. For all children, correct letter formation from the very beginning is the foundation for good handwriting.

*The child is referred to as she throughout this book; activities are equally suitable for boys and girls.

Capital letter formation

Copy these letters.

 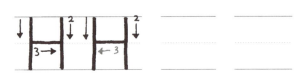

 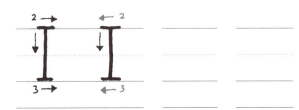

 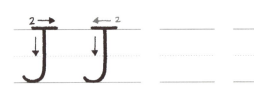

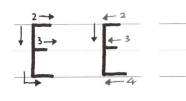 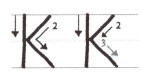

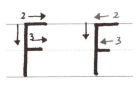 

B   S   M   T   B

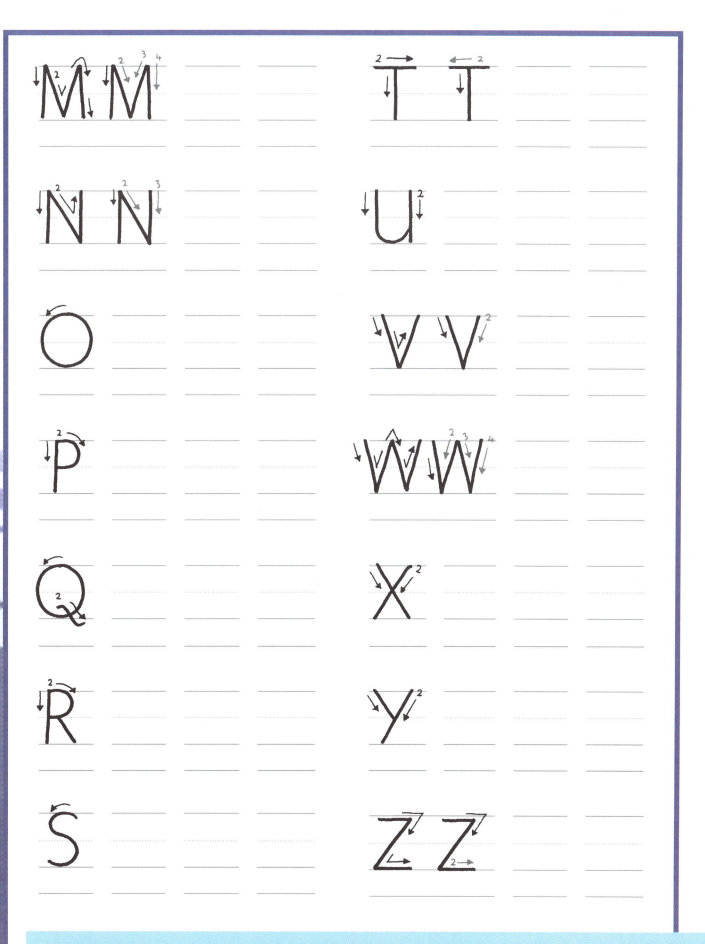

Labelling maps

His crew shout and yell and give him a shake
But nothing they do can make Pirate Snore wake.

Practise each word,
or part of a word, so that
you can help Pirate Snore
find the treasure.

an

pan

sand

land

bank

sank

in

fin

en

den

ten

on

pond

While Pirate Snore was asleep, one of his crew rubbed out some of the words on his treasure map. Choose the words from the lists and write them back in the correct place on the map.

Choose the correct word to write what the pirate crew are doing.

drink   plan   sing

The pirates _____

The pirates _____

The pirates _____

Use your skills

On a piece of paper draw and label your own treasure map.

Writing speech

If your tap is broken, with lots of drips and drops
And if you need a plumber, then send for Mrs Stops.

Practise each word
so that you can
help Mrs Stops.

get

jog

dog

job

pop

mop

shop

stop

drip

up

tap

six

fix

Help Mrs Stops tell you how she spends her day.
Fill in the missing words.

get
six

I ____ up
at ____.

jog
dog

I ____ with
my ____.

job

I drive
to the
____.

fix tap

I ____
the ____.

I ____ into
the ____.

pop
shop

stop drip

I ____
the ____.

mop up

I ____
____.

Use your skills

Write something you have done today.

Today I _____

_____

_____

_____

Instructions

Bring all your animals along to see the vet
You will find out what to do from kindly Mr Pet.

Practise each word so that you can help Mr Pet tell people how to look after their animals.

cat

rat

bat

dog

frog

keep

sheep

sleep

needs

Mr Pet has started to write some instructions for looking after the animals. Can you copy the words and help him to complete the instructions?

keep

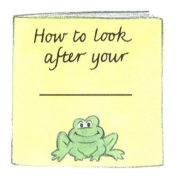

sleep

needs

_____ warm   let _____   _____ food

Mr Pet has lots of books to tell you how to look after your pet. Can you write the animal's name on its book?

How to look after your _____

How to look after your _____

How to look after your _____

How to look after your _____

How to look after your _____

Use your skills

Ask a grown-up to help you make your own book about the animals you like.
Write the names of the animals on the book cover.

Rhymes and messages

"I'm the fastest sailor that ever sailed the sea."
Captain Boast cries out," You won't catch me."

Practise each word so that you can help Captain Boast complete his rhyme.

rest

west

test

best

past

mast

last

fast

mist

gust

lost

Captain Boast is having a race. Copy the words to
complete his rhyme.

best   I am the very _____
test   I pass every _____
rest   I never take a _____
west   I sail from east to _____
mast   I climb up the _____
past   When other ships go _____
last   I tell them they'll be _____
fast   Because I go so _____ !

Copy the correct words to say why
he does not win.

gust   mist   lost

Captain Boast met a _____ of wind.

Captain Boast met _____.   Captain Boast got _____.

Use your skills

Write a message, asking for help, that Captain Boast can
put in a bottle.

_____
_____
_____

Captions and advertisements

If you see a flash of silver in the night sky
It may be Mrs Starlight flying by.

Practise each word, or part of a word, so that you can help Mrs Starlight with her rocket adventures.

one

zone

ome

home

ove

drove

ose

rose

ole

pole

oke

woke

smoke

clothes

Mrs Starlight is writing a book about her flight. Can you write the correct word in each space to complete the captions?

① clothes

Put on space _____

② zone

Went to takeoff _____

③ rose

Rocket _____ into sky

④ Smoke

_____ from booster rockets

⑤ Pole

Over South _____

⑥ Woke

_____ up among stars

⑦ Drove

_____ around planets

⑧ home

Back _____

Mrs Starlight writes lots of books.
Can you complete these titles for her?

Alone   pole

Home   jokes

Lunar Bookshop
Books by Mrs Starlight

_____ in space
_____ from the sky
Above the _____
Star _____

Parent point: Use extra paper to practise the words on page 14. Encourage your child to write captions for her own pictures and to have fun designing and writing advertisements.

Songs

Mr Bang the builder is busy all day long
If you pass close by, you'll hear him sing his song.

Practise each word so that you can help Mr Bang write the words of his song.

hitting	pushed
fitting	pulled
sitting	fetched
cutting	fixed
planning	mixed
dropping	mended

Mr Bang likes to sing as he works.
Write the words to complete his song.

planning
cutting

I'm _____, _____

hitting
dropping

I'm _____, _____

fitting
sitting

I'm _____, _____ .

pushed
pulled

I've _____ and _____

fetched
fixed

I've _____ and _____

mended
mixed

I've _____ and _____ .

Book titles

In Miss Check's classroom you'll find a book
That's just right for you if you just take a look.

Practise each word so that you can help Miss Check with her books.

girl

letter

circle

winter

birds

silver

birthday

spider

over

river

All the children in Miss Check's class have been writing books. They have drawn the pictures for the covers. Can you help them with the titles?

The Silver Spider
Birds in winter
A birthday letter
Girl in a circle
Over the river

Use your skills

Can you think of a good title for this book about the dirty monster?
Write it on the book cover.

Writing letters

Mr Breeze the beekeeper likes to show his bees
You can come and visit him near the nine pine trees.

Practise each word so that you can help Mr Breeze complete his letter.

nine		time
pine		like
prize		write
hive		white
arrive		invite
live		inside

Mr Breeze wants to invite the school children to visit. Help him to write the letter. Copy each word into the correct space.

like
invite
hives
prize
inside
white
hives
live
nine
Pine
write
time
arrive

9 Pine Tree Lane

Dear Miss Check

I would _____ to _____ your class to come and see my bee _____. The class will see the _____ honey the bees make _____ the _____ _____.

I _____ at number _____. _____ Tree Lane. Will you _____ to tell me the _____ you will _____?

Mr Breeze

Use your skills

Ask a grown up to help you write a letter to invite a friend to your house.

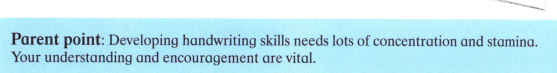

Parent point: Developing handwriting skills needs lots of concentration and stamina. Your understanding and encouragement are vital.

Posters

When Mr Smile the acrobat comes cycling into town
He likes to play the clown as he rides up and down.

Practise each word
so that you can help
Mr Smile with his poster.

side	seat
ride	treat
likes	ease
smile	please
quite	leaps

Mr Smile has to practise for his show and he has not had time to finish his poster. Please help him by copying the poem in the middle of the poster.

Mr Smile leaps with ease
Mr Smile likes to please
Take a seat
For quite a treat
And see him ride
From side to side!

Use your skills

Would you and your friends like to put on a show? Design a poster for your own show.

Parent point: When children know their handwriting will be displayed they are encouraged to do their best.

Diaries

Mr Harvest likes everything to be right
So he works on his farm from morning to night.

Practise each word
so that you can help
Mr Harvest to write
his diary.

more		order	
store		forget	
born		fork	
corn		sort	
morning		north	
stormy		important	

Mr Harvest has been so busy looking after the new foal that he has not had time to write his diary. Can you write this for him?

Sort important jobs

Monday

_____
_____
_____

Stormy night with north wind

Tuesday

_____
_____
_____

Check winter store

Wednesday

_____
_____
_____

Order more feed

Thursday

_____
_____
_____

Must not forget to mend fork

Friday
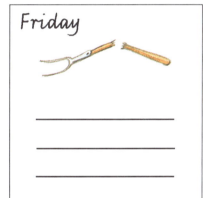

_____
_____
_____

Cut corn

Saturday

_____
_____
_____

New foal in the morning

Sunday

_____
_____
_____

Use your skills

Ask a grown-up to help you write your own diary for a week and draw the pictures.

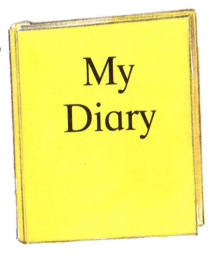

My Diary

Notes and menus

Mrs Taste says, "Come and try
My cheese flan, chips and cherry pie."

Practise each word so that you can help Mrs Taste plan her cooking.

chop

cherry

chill

kitchen

cheese

fish

chips

dishes

lunch

finish

fetch

mash

chicken

sharp

Mrs Taste has pinned some notes around the kitchen to help her remember what to do. Write in the words she has forgotten.

fetch

_____
vegetables

bunch

wash _____
of carrots

sharp

get _____ knife

chop

_____ onions

fish

cook _____

finish

_____
laying table

chill

_____ drinks

mash

_____ potatoes

dishes

wash _____

kitchen

clean _____

Use your skills

Write a menu for your favourite meal.
Ask a grown-up to help you list the words you need.

Notices and signs

Mrs Mow's garden shop opens every day
She has pretty plants to sell, and flowers on display.

Practise each word,
or part of a word,
so that you can
help Mrs Mow in
her garden shop.

ar	ay
car	pay
card	way
park	trays
sharp	spray
garden	today

Can you help Mrs Mow write some signs for her garden shop? Copy each word onto the correct sign.

park

car _____

cards

_____
for sale

today

open

_____ at

garden

_____ sprays

way

tools this _____

display

house plant
_____

trays

seed _____

sharp

_____
cutters

Use your skills

Draw a picture of Mrs Mow's shop.
Remember to write some signs.

Parent point: Use extra paper to practise the words on page 28. Writing their own signs and notices helps children to understand how important writing is in the world around them.

Stories

Mrs Track explores places far away
New people to see and adventures every day.

Practise each word so that you can help Mrs Track to write her story.

pack

truck

over

river

stormy

morning

forgot

important

rain

mountain

arrive

time

Mrs Track has come to talk to the children in Miss Check's class. She is telling them a story about her adventures. Can you write the story, using some of the words you have practised?

_____

_____

_____

_____

_____

_____

_____

_____

_____

Use your skills

You could use your best handwriting to make your own book of rhymes. Draw a picture of each person you have met in this book, and copy out the rhyme that goes with each person.

Parent point: Use extra paper to practise the words on page 30. Pin up your child's stories for all the family to enjoy.

The alphabet

A a   B b   C c   D d

E e   F f   G g   H h

I i   J j   K k   L l

M m   N n   O o   P p

Q q   R r   S s   T t

U u   V v   W w   X x

Y y   Z z